DATE DUE

MAY   2006

STEVEN SPIELBERG

TOM POWERS

In Consultation with Martha Cosgrove,
M.A. and Reading Specialist

JUST THE FACTS BIOGRAPHIES

LERNER PUBLICATIONS COMPANY/MINNEAPOLIS

Martha Cosgrove has a master's degree from the University of Minnesota in secondary education, with an emphasis on developmental and remedial reading. She is licensed in 7–12 English and language arts, developmental reading, and remedial reading. She has had several works published, and she gives numerous state and national presentations in her areas of expertise.

Lerner Publications Company
A division of Lerner Publishing Group
241 First Avenue North
Minneapolis, Minnesota U.S.A.

Website address: www.lernerbooks.com

Library of Congress Cataloging-in-Publication Data

Powers, Tom (Tom J.)
    Steven Spielberg / by Tom Powers.
        p.   cm. – (Just the facts bios)
    Includes bibliographical references and index.
    ISBN: 0-8225-2473-2 (lib. bdg. : alk. paper)
    1. Spielberg, Steven, 1946–Juvenile literature. 2. Motion picture
producers and directors–United States–Biography–Juvenile literature.
I. Title. II. Series.
PN1998.3.S65P69 2005
791.4302'33'092–dc22   2004014658

Manufactured in the United States of America
1 2 3 4 5 6 – JR – 10 09 08 07 06 05

CONTENTS

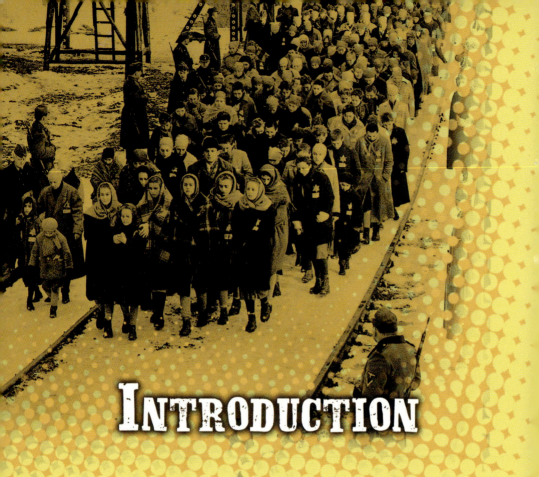

INTRODUCTION

(Above) In a scene from the movie *Schindler's List*, women enter the death camp called Auschwitz.

A SIGN HANGS across the entrance to the camp. In German, it says "Work will make you free. The sign is a lie. Nobody ever got out of this place. This is Auschwitz, a death camp created by Nazi Germany. More than one million people were murdered here during World War II (1939–1945).

In October of 1944, a train chugged through the countryside of southern Poland in eastern Europe. The train pulled a long line of train cars used to carry cattle. The train approached Auschwitz, with its brakes screeching. The powerful, surging engine slowed down. The train reached the outer yard of the camp, which was surrounded by thick walls and barbed-wire fences. The train then stopped.

Spotlights were aimed at the train from tall guard towers. Snarling dogs held tightly on leashes barked at the cattle cars. German soldiers wearing heavy overcoats stood with their rifles slung over their shoulders. Next to them stood prisoners wearing striped uniforms.

As soon as the train stopped, the prisoners moved forward. They flung open the train car doors and leaned wooden ramps on the edges. The cars were packed tightly—not with cattle, but with women. The women were Polish Jews. They didn't know it, but they had been brought to Auschwitz to be killed.

The women jumped down onto the ramps, then ran across the snow-covered yard. German guards herded the women toward a low door in a huge brick building. "Quickly, quickly," the guards yelled.

Then a voice pierced the night, and everything stopped. "Cut!" yelled the voice. Suddenly, the year was not 1944, but 1992. The women and the soldiers and the snarling dogs were only actors in a movie. The spotlights were movie lights. A camera moved through the air on a small crane. Assistants brought blankets and cups of coffee to shivering actors. The movie's director, Steven Spielberg, talked with the camera crew about filming the next scene. The movie was *Schindler's List.*

The movie tells the story of a group of Jews who survived the death camps of World War II. In the early 1940s, the Nazi government of Germany made a plan to kill all the Jews in Europe. The Nazis forced Jewish men, women, and children into concentration camps like Auschwitz. There they were starved, worked to death, shot, or gassed. Then their bodies were burned. The Nazis killed six million Jews and millions of other people. This mass murder came to be known as the Holocaust. (Holocaust actually means the destruction of people or animals by fire.)

A SERIOUS FILM

Like the victims in *Schindler's List,* Steven Spielberg is Jewish. In making a film about the Holocaust, he felt a strong sense of responsibility to the people who shared his faith. Millions of Jews around the world were counting on him to honor the memory of the dead. Spielberg had not always followed his religion closely. But he said that when he came to Poland to make his movie, "Jewish life came pouring back into my heart." Some of Spielberg's own family members came from the part of Poland where he filmed *Schindler's List.*

By 1992, Spielberg had become the most popular and financially successful filmmaker of all time. His films included *Jaws; E.T. the Extra-Terrestrial; Raiders of the Lost Ark;* and *Close Encounters of the Third Kind.* Audiences and movie critics liked his films. They had powerful acting and dazzling special effects.

But in a way, no one took Spielberg seriously. His movies made money—lots of money—but they didn't win awards. They didn't gain Spielberg the respect he wanted. People said that Spielberg made "kids' movies." They were movies about killer sharks and flying saucers and an action hero named Indiana Jones.

Not everyone believed that Steven Spielberg could make *Schindler's List.* They thought the story of the film was too serious for him. Spielberg asked for permission to film some scenes for *Schindler's List* inside Auschwitz. (The camp still stands in Poland.) Nine other movie crews had been given permission to film inside the camp. Spielberg's request, however, was denied. The director was told that the camp was a holy place and a memorial to those who had died there. The denial suggested that maybe Spielberg wasn't a serious enough director to work inside Auschwitz.

> **IT'S A FACT!**
> Jerzy Wroblewski— the museum director who wouldn't allow Spielberg to film in Auschwitz—had had bad experiences with past film crews. Wroblewski believed that the thousands of extras would destroy the historic site.

Spielberg himself admitted that he had never wanted to make movies about pain and suffering. "I've often protected myself with the movie camera," Spielberg said. "The camera has always been my golden shield against things really reaching me."

To make *Schindler's List,* Spielberg had to look deep inside himself. He had to ask himself if he was a serious filmmaker. In the past, he had made movies about escapes and fantasies and adventures, about brave children and foolish parents. Could he deal with the horrible reality of the Holocaust? To make *Schindler's List,* Spielberg had to use all the skills he had learned during twenty years as a filmmaker. He also had to think about things he feared and things he loved and valued most. He had to overcome his own doubts about making such a serious film. Was he ready?

1

THE WEIRD, SKINNY KID

STEVEN SPIELBERG was born December 18, 1946, in Cincinnati, Ohio. He was the oldest of four children—himself and three sisters—born to Arnold and Leah Spielberg. Arnold was an electrical engineer who helped design the first computers. His father's job required frequent moves. So Steven grew up in several states, including New Jersey, Arizona, and California.

(Above)
Steven with his father Arnold

Arnold Spielberg shared his love of science and astronomy with his son. He hoped Steven would pursue a career in science. Once, when Steven was six years old, his father woke him up late at night. Together, they drove into the countryside to watch a meteor shower. The meteor was a huge rock that was breaking up as it sped toward Earth. Pieces of rock from space burned and streaked across the sky. Steven treasured that moment.

Arnold Spielberg encouraged his son to work hard at his math and science classes. Spielberg inherited a love of science fiction from his father. But he didn't have the desire to become a scientist.

His mother is probably the person who showed Steven how to use all his talents. Leah Spielberg was trained as a classical pianist. Classical music is traditional music with European roots that can be hard to play. She often invited other female musicians to the house to play classical music. Steven's father was often away on business. "I was raised in a world of women," Spielberg said. "Even the dog was female."

Spielberg's father had little interest in classical music. His passion was computers, and he spent long hours at his job. Leah Spielberg was much more playful than her husband was. Over the years,

IT'S A FACT!

As an adult, Steven praised his parents for doing such a good job of raising him and his sisters, even as their marriage was failing.

Steven with his mother, Leah *(center)*, and sister Sue *(left)*

Arnold and Leah Spielberg grew apart. They had few interests in common. Only their love for their children held the marriage together.

CHILDHOOD FEARS

Steven loved to torment his little sisters—Sue, Anne, and Nancy. Once he locked them inside a closet, where he had rigged a ghostly skeleton with a light glowing in its eye socket. Another time, he cut off the head of Nancy's favorite doll. Then he placed it on a bed of lettuce, surrounded it with tomato slices, and served it to her on a platter. Steven himself was frightened by quite a few things–dark closets and spooky trees and bathtubs with feet. But he learned that he could beat his own fears by making his sisters even more scared than he was.

Steven loved movies and television, and Walt Disney films were his favorite. Disney probably influenced Spielberg more than any other filmmaker. Spielberg has said that he was more frightened by the scary creatures and music in the "Night on Bald Mountain" sequence in *Fantasia* than by anything else he ever saw in the movies. A lot of other things frightened Steven when he was a little boy. A television documentary on snakes made him cry. The death of Bambi's mother in *Bambi* left him shaken. Steven covered his eyes and burst into tears when the wicked queen in Disney's *Snow White and the Seven Dwarfs* turned into a skeleton and crumbled into pieces. He was even afraid of the dark. "The first scary thing I learned to do as a child," he said, "was turn off the light!"

Spielberg did not give in to his fears, though. He may have gone to bed afraid, but he woke up brave. "In the morning I was the bravest guy–there was little seven-year-old Steven walking around the closet, saying 'I'm not afraid of you.' Or talking to the trees and clouds, saying 'I'm not afraid of you.' But once night fell, all bets were off."

Years later, Spielberg made use of his childhood fears in directing his movies. Most of his films contain powerful, scary figures: a killer truck, a giant shark, a raging forest fire, wicked pirates, evil Nazis. Spielberg shares his fears with audiences. "I like to feel my skin crawling," he said. "I'm diabolical [evil] in that sense. I get . . . pleasure in making people sweat in their underwear. It doesn't make me the nicest guy in the world but I sure enjoy it."

But there is always a "little guy" in Spielberg's films who wins over fear and evil. Sometimes the "little guy" is an ordinary man or woman. Sometimes it's a child who must conquer fear and take action, just like young Steven Spielberg.

YOUNG MOVIEMAKER

Steven spent the late 1950s and early 1960s in Scottsdale, Arizona, a suburb of Phoenix. In school, other students thought Spielberg was a wimp. "I was the weird skinny kid with acne," he says. He was poor at sports and games. When he was told to cut up a frog in biology class, he threw up. Steven's father allowed him to start making family movies because he wanted his son to become more self-confident.

Steven soon took over the house with his moviemaking. He turned the family living room into a movie studio. It was cluttered with electrical cables and powerful lights. He was so excited about making movies that he never seemed to leave his family alone. According to Spielberg's mother, her son did not understand the meaning of the word *no*.

Spielberg got his mother and sisters and friends to act in his films. Spielberg's mother was happy to help. She helped him make costumes for his films. She drove him into the Arizona desert when he wanted to film "on location." She cooked thirty cans of cherries so that he could film the blood-red glop for scary special effects. Spielberg has said that his mother was like a "big kid," full of fun and enthusiasm for his projects.

Steven Spielberg made his first movie, called *Battle Squad*, in 1960. It was about fighting Nazis,

IT'S A FACT!

In fourth grade, Spielberg joined the band and orchestra at his school. He played the clarinet.

and he was thirteen years old. Steven filmed it with a small camera that his mother had given to his father for Father's Day.

Steven made an interesting choice for the star of his movie. He chose a large boy who liked to beat up Steven and let the air out of his bicycle tires. Steven told the bully that he was making a film about soldiers fighting the Nazis in World War II. He wanted him to play the hero. The boy laughed in Spielberg's face. But Steven kept asking, and finally, the bully agreed.

Steven dressed his new star in a helmet, backpack, and soldier's clothes. He tried to make him look like movie star John Wayne. By the time they had finished shooting *Battle Squad,* the former bully had become Spielberg's best friend.

From the age of thirteen on, Spielberg knew that he wanted to be a filmmaker. He realized that the movie camera could be his "golden shield." It was his protection against bullies at school, against trouble at home, against every fear, real or imagined.

At Arcadia High School in Phoenix, Steven joined the theater arts program. He found that he had choices besides being a popular athlete or a weird, skinny kid. When he was fifteen, he made his biggest film yet. It was a two-and-a-half-hour science fiction epic called *Firelight*. The film cost five hundred dollars and took a year to make, mainly because Steven could only film on weekends. To raise money for the film, he worked after school. He filmed it with a small, 8-millimeter camera. (Professional movies are shot on film that is 35 millimeters wide. The wider the film is, the sharper the images are and the brighter the colors.) When *Firelight* was finished, Steven persuaded a Phoenix movie theater owner to let him show it. The film's "world premier" took place on March 24,

It's a Fact!

When he was twelve, Spielberg rented 8-millimeter movies and charged kids thirty-five cents to watch them at his house. He got dozens of customers. Today, FBI warnings at the beginning of each rented film clearly tell viewers this practice is illegal.

1963. Spielberg charged admission and ended up making fifty dollars more than the film had cost him.

SEMI-UNHAPPY

Shortly after his triumph with *Firelight,* Steven's family moved from Phoenix to Saratoga, California. The city is a suburb of San Jose, where the computer industry was booming. In Saratoga, Spielberg felt the sting of anti-Semitism (hatred of Jews) for the first time. Spielberg grew up with a strong awareness of his Jewish heritage. His parents and grandparents were often visited by friends and relatives who had survived the Holocaust in Germany.

In Arizona, Steven's classmates made fun of him because they thought he was weird, not because he was Jewish. But in 1964, his last year in high school, Spielberg was treated badly because of his religion. In study hall, classmates threw things at him. Other students called him cruel names that made fun of his religion and tried to beat him up.

While Steven was in high school, the Spielberg family was going through a hard time. Soon after they moved to California, Arnold and Leah Spielberg divorced. Steven Spielberg has said that for him *divorce* was the ugliest word in the English

**Spielberg in his junior
year of high school**

language. He and his
sisters held each other
and cried when they
heard their parents
arguing and talking
about divorce.

Spielberg has
called his childhood
"semi-unhappy."
There were too many
moves. Too many arguments blew up between his
serious father and his fun-loving mother. Spielberg
said that the tension between his parents was "not
violence, just . . . unhappiness you could cut with a
fork." He responded by losing himself in films and
television and making his own movies. For him,
movies were an escape, where he could create and
experience the warm family life that he'd missed.

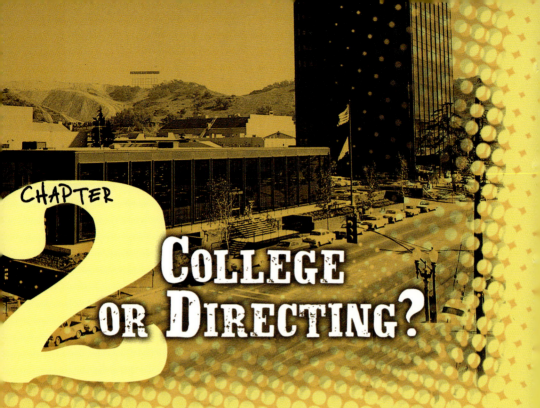

CHAPTER 2

COLLEGE OR DIRECTING?

AFTER GRADUATING from high school, Spielberg hoped to study filmmaking in college. He tried several times to get into the top college film programs. But they wouldn't accept him because his high school grades were too low. Spielberg was embarrassed by his low high school grades, which were partly due to his poor reading skills. As a child, Spielberg read comic books rather than literature. He spent more time watching movies and television than he did reading. He later wished he had made himself a stronger reader.

(Above) **Universal Studios in Los Angeles, California**

Eventually, Spielberg enrolled as an English major at California State University. The school was in Long Beach, near Los Angeles. During the summer before college, Spielberg took a tour of Universal Studios in Los Angeles. The studios were one of the main places for making movies. He wandered away from the tour and talked with the men and women who made movies at Universal. The next day, Spielberg returned to the studio. He wore a suit and carried a briefcase. He simply walked into the studio looking like an important person. The guards at the front gate didn't stop him.

Every day that summer, Spielberg, dressed in a suit and tie, explored the Universal grounds, called the lot. He talked with directors, writers, and editors. Eventually, he found an office that wasn't being used and moved in. He bought plastic letters and put his name—Steven Spielberg, Room 22C—in the list of people who worked in the building. No one caught him.

Spielberg often sneaked onto sets where movies were being made. One day, he got to see one of his heroes in action. The director Alfred Hitchcock was making a film called *Torn Curtain*. Spielberg greatly

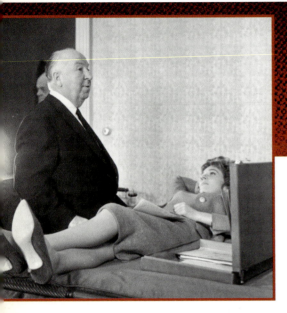

Alfred Hitchcock directs Julie Andrews on the set of *Torn Curtain*.

admired the large, quiet English director known as "the master of suspense." Hitchcock knew how to build tension in a scene. Hitchcock's audiences were frightened and delighted at the same time. Spielberg jumped at the chance to see Hitchcock at work. Unfortunately, a Universal security guard discovered Spielberg and threw him off the Hitchcock set.

First Film

Spielberg continued to visit Universal Studios even after he began taking college classes. He pestered studio executives into watching his 8-millimeter movies. One of the Universal producers finally told Spielberg that he would have to spend more money on his films. He said Steven had to use a 35-millimeter camera if he really wanted to impress anybody. Spielberg's 8-millimeter films looked small, blurry, and dull when they were projected onto a big screen.

Movie Terms

crosscut: to move back and forth between two different scenes that are happening at the same time

director: the person who is responsible for what a movie looks like on screen. The director is in charge of actors, sets, camera placement, and other things that make a movie look the way it does.

editor: a person who rearranges each piece of approved film to make a movie flow better

extra: a person who is hired to act in a scene as part of a large group of people

feature: a motion picture that is long (usually an hour and a half to two hours) and important enough to be shown in movie theaters

lead role: the most important role in a movie

producer: the person who takes care of the business of making a movie. This mostly means getting money for the movie and making sure it gets made.

set: the scenery for a play or movie

supporting role: a role in a movie that is the second-most important role after the lead role(s)

Spielberg had a friend named Denis Hoffman who wanted to produce movies. (A producer takes care of getting the money to make a movie. The director is in charge of the actors and the look of the movie.) In 1968, Hoffman agreed to give Spielberg fifteen thousand dollars to direct a twenty-two-minute, 35-millimeter film. The director was twenty-one.

The film, called *Amblin'*, was about a young couple hitchhiking from the desert to the Pacific Ocean. To keep the film simple, Spielberg told the story without anyone talking in the movie. He filmed *Amblin'* in ten days and added music and sound effects after the film was shot.

Spielberg now calls *Amblin'* a "slick" film and compares it to "a Pepsi commercial." But the short film served its purpose. It showed people that Steven Spielberg could make a high-quality, professional-looking movie. The executives at Universal Studios were impressed.

The day after *Amblin'* was shown at Universal, Spielberg was called into the office of Sidney Sheinberg. Sheinberg was Universal's head of television production. "Sir, I like your work," Sheinberg said. "How would you like to go to work professionally?"

SEEING *AMBLIN'*

Universal purchased the rights to show *Amblin'* in movie theaters. The short film was paired with *Love Story*, one of the most popular feature films of 1970. Years later, when Spielberg started his own production company, he named it Amblin Entertainment. *Amblin'* was the movie that launched his professional career.

"But I have a year left to go in college," Spielberg said.

"Kid," Sheinberg said, "do you want to go to college or do you want to direct?"

Spielberg had wanted to become a movie director since he was thirteen years old. He could not let the chance slip by. In 1969, he signed a seven-year contract to direct television shows and movies for Universal. "I quit college so fast, I didn't even clean out my locker," Spielberg said.

Sidney Sheinberg became Spielberg's mentor. As a mentor, he provided the young filmmaker with guidance

IT'S A FACT!

When Spielberg received a Lifetime Achievement Award from the American Film Institute in 1995, Sidney Sheinberg presented it to him.

Spielberg and his mentor, Sidney Sheinberg

and advice. Over time, he gave Spielberg the chance to direct more important motion pictures.

TELEVISION DIRECTOR

Spielberg's first assignment at Universal was to direct an episode for a weekly science fiction TV series called *Night Gallery*. Spielberg directed a story called "Eyes." It was written by Rod Serling. Serling had created both *Night Gallery* and another popular science fiction television series, *The Twilight Zone*.

"Eyes" starred old-time screen legend Joan Crawford. Spielberg was five-foot-six and boyish looking at twenty-two. He was afraid that a famous star like Crawford would not listen to his directions. Instead, Crawford treated Spielberg with respect. She asked for his advice on how to play her role, and she followed his directions. Just to keep on the star's good side, Spielberg brought Crawford a rose every day.

In "Eyes," Crawford plays a wealthy New Yorker who has gone blind. She desperately wants to see again, even if only for a short time. She meets a man who has just been told by doctors that his eyes will be able to see for just a few more hours. The woman gives the

Joan Crawford starred in the first episode of *Night Gallery* that Spielberg directed.

man a lot of money in exchange for his eyes. Surgeons put his eyes into the woman. Just as her bandages are removed, the whole world goes dark.

IT'S A FACT!

The New York blackout of 1965 left about thirty million people without power. It was the largest power failure until the 2003 blackout, which hit fifty million people.

New York City has gone into a power failure—the famous blackout of 1965. The woman's new eyes will fail before the lights come back on.

"Eyes" aired on television on November 8, 1969. Spielberg went on to direct other episodes of *Night Gallery.* He also directed episodes of *Marcus Welby, M.D.; The Night of the Game; The Psychiatrists;* and *Columbo.* As a television director, Spielberg learned how to work quickly and how to meet a budget. "TV taught me to think on my feet," he said.

Spielberg also learned to tell stories in a short time. In a television episode, there's not a lot of time to explain things to an audience. Working on television shows, Spielberg became a skilled filmmaker and a clever storyteller.

FEATURE FILMS

Working in television, Spielberg didn't have much freedom to experiment. He wanted to put his camera in unusual places or move it in complicated ways. But he soon learned that television shows had to be filmed in a straightforward manner. They are made according to a formula set down by the studios.

For Spielberg, television direction was no longer an art form. It was just a job. After two years, he grew tired of directing television shows. He wanted to make "features." These are motion pictures that are big enough, long enough, and important enough to be shown in movie theaters. He had five more years before his contract was finished. And, under his contract, he had to take the assignments he was given. He couldn't choose what to work on. His breakthrough came with *Duel,* a 1971 movie made for television. With *Duel,* Spielberg rediscovered the fun of filmmaking.

Spielberg's first feature-length film was filled with suspense. *Duel* is a simple story about a salesman named David Mann. Mann is driving through central California on a business trip. On the highway, Mann is behind a huge truck that won't let him pass. When he finally manages to zip past the "road hog," the truck begins to tailgate him. Then the truck driver tries to run him off the road. Mann never gets a good look at the truck driver. It seems like the giant truck itself is trying to kill him. No matter what Mann does, the truck is right behind him, slamming into his car, trying to run him over. Finally, after many narrow escapes, the truck and car lock together and drive over a cliff. Mann survives by jumping free at the last second.

Duel was filmed in sixteen days in the California desert on a budget of $425,000. Spielberg asked an artist to draw the whole story on a long strip of paper. He hung this drawing on the wall in his desert motel room, running it all the way around the room. This way, Spielberg could see the whole movie at once.

IT'S A FACT!

The storyboard process was invented in 1931 by Webb Smith, a Disney employee. Walt Disney insisted on seeing complete storyboards for all proposed cartoons, movies, TV shows, and even amusement park rides.

He could think about what part of it he wanted to film each day. "Storyboarding"—sketching action sequences or entire films on paper—became an important tool for Spielberg. With a storyboard, he could come to the set every day fully prepared, knowing just what scenes he wanted to film.

Duel was so popular on American television that Universal decided to release it in movie theaters in Europe. The film's story is told largely through action, not words, so audiences in any country could enjoy it. As a result of *Duel,* Spielberg became a well-known director in Europe even before he became famous in the United States.

With the success of *Duel,* Spielberg got the chance to direct a major motion picture. This 1974 film, *The Sugarland Express,* was not popular with audiences, but it was well made. The film involved another kind of car chase. This time, a whole string of police cars chases a young woman and her husband across the plains of Texas. The couple makes a jailbreak and kidnaps a police officer as they head for the town of Sugarland. They want to get their baby back from a foster family. One Texas officer tries to bring the couple in safely, but in the end, the husband is shot and killed by police.

The Sugarland Express convinced Universal executives that Spielberg could handle important movie projects. Spielberg had taken a large crew to Texas, where he spent sixty days filming. He was able to get a strong, serious performance from his star, Goldie Hawn, who acted mainly in funny TV shows and movies. He filmed huge car crashes destroying 50 cars. He staged scenes with 240 cars and 5,000 extras. Steven's work on *The Sugarland Express* put his directing career in high gear.

Goldie Hawn *(left)* and Michael Sachs *(right)* on the set of *The Sugarland Express*

CHAPTER 3
THE BLOCKBUSTER YEARS

(Above) A scene with the killer shark from *Jaws*

ON THE BASIS OF *The Sugarland Express,* Universal Studios assigned Spielberg to direct *Jaws,* a scary story about a killer shark. *Jaws* (released in 1975) was the most difficult film Spielberg had ever tried to make.

Jaws is the story of a giant shark that attacks people in the northeastern United States. The town's chief of police, played by Roy Schieder, teams up with a young scientist, played by Richard Dreyfuss, and an old shark hunter to search for the beast and kill it. But the shark sinks the hunters' boat and eats one of the men. The police chief saves himself by wedging an oxygen tank into the monster's mouth.

As the boat sinks, the chief clings to its mast, a few feet above the water. Out on the ocean, the great shark rushes toward him once more. The chief fires his gun at the tank in the shark's mouth. The tank explodes, blowing the shark to bits.

Spielberg filmed *Jaws* on the island of Martha's Vineyard, off the coast of Massachusetts. The production had many problems. Three different mechanical sharks were built for the film. They were all difficult to operate. They sank, their fake skin peeled off, and their control systems exploded. Filming on the sea created more problems.

WHO NEEDS BIG STARS?

Spielberg found that it wasn't always necessary to use big stars. Famous actors can call too much attention to themselves in a TV show or a movie. Even after Spielberg became famous, he liked to use good actors who were not very well known. He cast the young Richard Dreyfuss as the hero in *Jaws* and *Close Encounters of the Third Kind.* He thought Dreyfuss had a special talent for playing the underdog, the little guy who wins out against great odds.

Pleasure boats got in the way. Scenes filmed one day on a glassy sea did not match scenes filmed the next day when the sea was rough. Crew members were injured in strange accidents. Actor Richard Dreyfuss was heard to mutter, "If any of us had any sense, we'd all bail out now."

Dreyfuss was joking. He trusted Spielberg to get the film made no matter how long it took. The production schedule allowed fifty-two days for shooting on Martha's Vineyard. The actual filming took three times that long. Cast and crew members sometimes left the island to take a break from the filming. But Spielberg refused to leave Martha's Vineyard. He said he was afraid that if he left, he would never come back.

The cost of the film doubled and then tripled. Executives at Universal Studios asked producers David Brown and Richard Zanuck to either replace Spielberg or cancel the whole project. The producers refused.

IT'S A FACT!

Critics praised Spielberg for making *Jaws* scarier by not showing the shark. In reality, shots of the shark were taken out of the movie because the mechanical shark often didn't work.

Actor Roy Scheider *(left)*, producer Richard Zanuck *(center)*, and director Spielberg *(right)* take a break on the set of *Jaws*.

Sidney Sheinberg–Universal's new president and Steven's old mentor–backed them up. Sheinberg had looked at the film's "rushes," the scenes Spielberg had already completed. Sheinberg saw that Spielberg was making a terrific movie.

THE FIRST BLOCKBUSTER

Jaws was finally completed and released to movie theaters in June 1975. It became the first Hollywood movie to take in more than $100 million at the box office. *Jaws* was the first blockbuster movie. Because *Jaws* earned so much money, it changed the way many producers thought about filmmaking. Producers no longer wanted to find the money to make several small, well-made films. Instead, they now hoped to make one hugely successful blockbuster. A single hit like *Jaws* could mean wealth and power for the people who made it. Film studios began to spend more and more money on movies, hoping to hit the jackpot with a blockbuster. By the late 1970s, the fate of an entire studio could depend on the success or failure of a single movie.

Most movies that become blockbusters have certain specific parts. The story must be clear and the characters fairly simple. This makes the movie easy for younger viewers and foreign audiences to follow. These are the viewers who will pay to see an exciting movie like *Jaws* two or three times.

IT'S A FACT!

A blockbuster originally described a very large bomb that could clear an entire block. The word has come to mean anything that is large and successful.

A blockbuster needs thrills so audiences will want to see the movie again and again. Most blockbusters move at a fast pace, with exciting action and lots of special effects. A blockbuster movie is designed like a roller-coaster ride.

Jaws set the pattern for blockbuster movies. The film did not have big stars, but it had a well-told story. It had exciting action, beating music, and eye-popping special effects. Universal Studios gave *Jaws* a powerful advertising campaign. The movie's poster shows the tiny figure of a woman swimming in the ocean. In the water below her looms a killer shark, as big as a house. *Jaws* was also one of the first movies that was widely promoted on television.

SPIELBERG AND LUCAS

Some critics blamed Spielberg for bringing about a new era in Hollywood. The critics admitted Spielberg had made movies more exciting. But he also made them less serious. Spielberg liked the same kind of simple but thrilling movies that mass audiences like. And he made those movies better than anybody else. He became successful as a filmmaker because he shared the tastes of the viewers who paid to see his films.

By the 1970s, many people felt that Hollywood had lost touch with its audience. In particular, the studios did not seem to know what younger viewers wanted to see. As a result, the studios turned to young filmmakers like Spielberg and Lucas for new ideas.

MEETING GEORGE

Spielberg first met George Lucas at the screening of *THX 1138: 4EB*. This was a short science fiction film that Lucas made while attending film school. Spielberg saw in Lucas a "kindred spirit," someone who shared his passion and talent for filmmaking. "He reminded me a little bit of Walt Disney's version of a mad scientist," Spielberg said. Over the years, Lucas and Spielberg became filmmaking partners and close friends.

Lucas *(left)* and Spielberg

More than any other filmmakers of the time, Spielberg and Lucas helped reshape Hollywood. Lucas made his first hit film, *American Graffiti*, in 1973. It used young actors and rock-and-roll music to appeal to young audiences. Before *American Graffiti*, Hollywood movies had rarely used rock-and-roll songs in their sound tracks. The success of this film created a pattern for sound tracks that movies have followed ever since.

Lucas went on to make the *Star Wars* trilogy. These were three fantasy films that young audiences loved. While Lucas was directing the first *Star Wars* saga, Spielberg was making his own science fiction film, *Close Encounters of the Third Kind* (released in 1977).

In *Close Encounters,* a group of ordinary people from all around the country are drawn to one spot near Devils Tower in Wyoming. Their friends and families think they have gone crazy. But the people find a wonderful surprise at the end of their journey. A huge, bright spaceship filled with gentle beings arrives from outer space. For one scene in the movie, Spielberg used his childhood memory of seeing a meteor shower with his father to create a scene with beautiful streaking lights in the sky.

Many people in Hollywood were angry at and jealous of Spielberg for becoming so successful before he was thirty years old. "All it took was *Jaws* to be this big hit in 1975," Spielberg said, "and then there were some people who went after *Close Encounters of the Third Kind* as if I had murdered their entire family."

1

E.T. PHONE HOME

AFTER THE BLOCKBUSTER SUCCESS of *Jaws* and *Close Encounters,* Spielberg experienced his first major failure. He tried to make another blockbuster and it bombed. In 1979, Spielberg directed a World War II comedy called *1941.* The film was about a Japanese submarine that fired on an oil refinery along the coast of California. The story was based on a real event from the war.

Spielberg's film showed the comic parts of the event. There were confused Japanese sailors, wacky U.S. pilots, and mixed-up civilian patrols. The film included a large cast, complicated crowd scenes, and expensive special effects. Its budget soared to $40 million. But the slapstick humor that Spielberg hoped to achieve got lost in the huge film. *Newsweek* critic David Ansen wrote, "Somewhere inside this bloated epic a slim [movie] is screaming to be heard." Audiences felt worn out by the film rather than amused or entertained.

THE ADVENTURES OF INDIANA JONES

After *1941* flopped at the box office, Spielberg needed to restart his career. He found a sure hit in *Raiders of the Lost Ark* (1981). This was an adventure movie directed by Spielberg and produced by George Lucas. *Raiders* was the first of three films that featured the character Indiana Jones. "Indy," played by actor Harrison Ford, is a mild-mannered college professor. He leads a double life as a two-fisted, whip-snapping archaeologist.

In *Raiders of the Lost Ark,* he fights Nazis to gain control over the biblical Ark of the Covenant. In other adventures, Indy travels to India to recover stones sacred to the Hindu religion

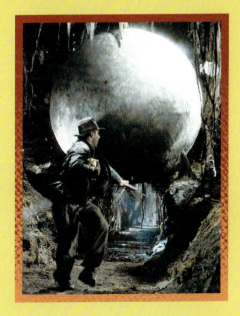

A scene from *Raiders of the Lost Ark*

(Indiana Jones and the Temple of Doom, 1984) and battles Nazis again in a search for the Holy Grail *(Indiana Jones and the Last Crusade,* 1989).

Indiana Jones became one of the most popular movie heroes of the 1980s. Audiences took comfort in an old-fashioned hero like Indiana Jones. They felt good cheering for an "ordinary guy" who uses his fists and his wits to survive. Throughout the 1980s, the adventures of Indiana Jones helped Spielberg remain Hollywood's most popular filmmaker.

While he was filming *Raiders of the Lost Ark,* Spielberg worked out the idea for *E.T.* At first, Spielberg thought he wanted to make a movie about aliens invading Earth. It would be a scary sequel to *Close Encounters of the Third Kind.* He wrote a story called "Night Skies" and asked writer-director John Sayles to develop it as a screenplay. When Spielberg saw Sayles's treatment of the story, he liked one small, friendly alien more than the other hostile invaders. He began to focus on the friendly alien. "What if he got left behind?" Spielberg wondered. "What if the little chap, the straggler, missed the bus home?"

Spielberg was shooting *Raiders* on location in Tunisia, North Africa, when screenwriter Melissa Mathison arrived to visit actor Harrison Ford.

Melissa Mathison and Harrison Ford

(Mathison and Ford were later married.) Mathison had cowritten the screenplay for *The Black Stallion* (1979), a polished and popular children's movie produced by Francis Ford Coppola. Since then, she had grown frustrated with screenwriting. She had turned down an earlier offer to work on *E.T.* But Spielberg got Mathison interested in his new ideas about the story of a stranded alien. Together, they began to work out the details of E.T.'s adventure. Mathison returned to the United States to write the screenplay.

E.T. THE EXTRATERRESTRIAL

To design the lovable extraterrestrial for *E.T.*, Spielberg hired Carlo Rambaldi. Rambaldi was a

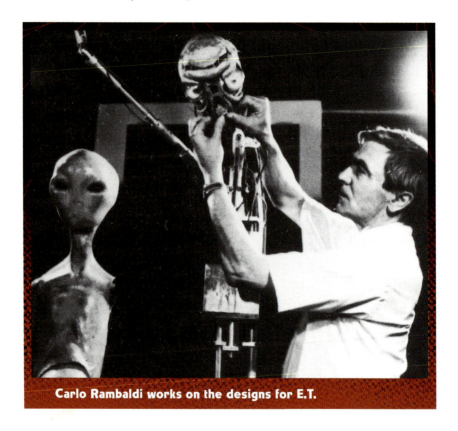

Carlo Rambaldi works on the designs for E.T.

sculptor who had created a giant ape for *King Kong* (1976) and a big-headed monster for *Alien* (1979). Rambaldi and his coworkers spent more than five thousand hours creating three versions of E.T. They built a mechanical model that could walk by itself. They built an electronic model whose face muscles could be operated by remote control. And they built an E.T. "suit" that was worn by several small actors, including a boy who had been born without legs. E.T.'s voice was provided by Pat Welsh, a woman in her sixties. Actress Debra Winger added vocal effects. Spielberg hired an old friend, Allen Daviau, to be director of photography. Filming began in September of 1981, and the movie was finished and released to theaters the following June.

E.T. is the story of a ten-year-old boy named Elliott who finds a creature from outer space in his backyard. Elliott does not have many friends.

PAYBACK

E.T.'s director of photography was Allen Daviau (right). Years before, Daviau had worked for low pay as the cameraman on Amblin'. Spielberg had promised Daviau that someday they would make feature films together. In 1981, Daviau was filming television commercials. Then Spielberg, repaying the old debt, asked him to film E.T. After E.T., Daviau found a lot of work in Hollywood. He worked again with Spielberg as director of photography on The Color Purple and Empire of the Sun.

His older brother has little time for him. His younger sister is a pest. His mother always seems frantic, trying to work at a job and raise three kids at the same time.

Elliott's father does not live with the family. As in many Spielberg films, the missing father is an important theme in *E.T.* Like many Spielberg heroes, Elliott wants to find a "father figure," a strong man who can take care of those weaker than himself. In some ways, Elliott even tries to become a father figure to the extraterrestrial, or "E.T.," who has been left behind by his spaceship.

At first, Elliott treats E.T. like a child. Elliott teaches the little creature about candy and television and comic books. Elliott rescues E.T. from danger. Then, as the film progresses, Elliott and E.T. learn to be brave together. They share comic

IT'S A FACT!

In the original script for *E.T.*, the alien ate M&Ms instead of Reese's Pieces. The Mars Company, which makes M&Ms, didn't want their candy in the film. They thought E.T. was ugly and would scare children. Reese's Pieces sales increased 65 percent thanks to this movie.

adventures. They go trick-or-treating together, and they accidentally get drunk on beer.

Finally, E.T. becomes a kind of father to Elliott. The little space being is really old and wise. He teaches Elliott that the bravest thing anyone can do is to love somebody else. Early in the film, E.T. learns to say "ouch" when he hurts his finger. At the end of the film, when E.T.'s spaceship returns for him, he says "ouch" again. This time, he says it

Spielberg poses with his famous extraterrestrial.

for the pain he feels in his heart. Elliott and E.T. have learned to feel the same things, and the strongest feeling is love.

Critics and audiences praised *E.T.* for its style as well as its story. Spielberg placed lights behind the characters so they seemed to glow with power and mystery. This "backlighting" was something that Spielberg had worked on for years. With *E.T.*, it became a trademark of his style.

E.T. was so popular with audiences that an image and a line of dialogue from the film entered American popular culture. The line occurs when E.T. builds a machine to contact his own planet. "E.T. phone home," the alien tells Elliott. That line became a popular saying in the 1980s.

PHONING HOME

Many critics have noted that Spielberg's films often have a "longing for home" theme. The space alien E.T. yearns to return home to his planet. The shark hunters in *Jaws* sing a song, "Show Me the Way to Go Home," as they await their final battle with the shark. Spielberg has said that the "longing for home" theme in his movies comes from his own childhood memories.

The famous bicycle flight from *E.T.*

The most famous image from *E.T.* comes at the end of the film. Elliott and the neighborhood boys are racing on their bicycles to return E.T. to his spaceship. They are being chased by police cars and government vans. The boys cut across parks and vacant lots, but finally they are trapped. At that point, E.T. uses his superhuman powers to send the bicycles flying through the air. Elliott, who is carrying E.T. in a basket on the front of his bicycle, soars into the sky. That image—the outline of a boy flying across the moon—was deeply moving to viewers. Spielberg gave people a reminder of what it means to dream with the heart of a child.

5

SUCCESSES AND SETBACKS

RAIDERS OF THE LOST ARK, *E.T.,* and *Indiana Jones and the Temple of Doom* gave Spielberg three smash hits in a row. Despite his popularity, Spielberg had many setbacks in the 1980s. As the character Indiana Jones once said, "It's not the years that kill you, it's the mileage." During the 1980s, Spielberg traveled down some bumpy roads. The journey did not kill him, but it made him wiser.

THE TWILIGHT ZONE

In 1982, Spielberg coproduced and codirected a movie based on the old television series *The Twilight Zone*. Spielberg's contribution to *Twilight Zone–The Movie* was an episode called "Kick the Can." In "Kick the Can," a group of bored, unhappy senior citizens begin to play a simple children's game.

Magically, they become children again. Spielberg spent just six days filming the story. He made the short film quickly because he wanted to get away from the whole *Twilight Zone* project. Disaster had struck one of *Twilight Zone*'s other episodes.

Spielberg's coproducer, John Landis, was directing the biggest and most expensive of *Twilight Zone*'s four stories. In the Landis story, actor Vic Morrow plays a bigot, a man who hates people who are different from him. Leaving a bar one night, the bigot steps into the "Twilight Zone." He finds himself tumbling through time, popping up in one place and then another. In each place, he is treated cruelly by other bigots. He is a Jew in Nazi Germany. He is an African American who is nearly killed by a mob of white people. And he is a Vietnamese soldier who must save a pair of children from a frightening helicopter attack.

IT'S A FACT!

The *Twilight Zone* was a TV show that ran from 1959 to 1965. New versions of the show also appeared in the 1980s and briefly in 2002. This show was one of the few that succeeded in featuring a different cast of characters in each episode.

During the filming of the helicopter attack, Landis insisted on everything being as real as possible. He brought two young children to a rugged location late at night. This action broke child labor laws, which said when and how kids could work. He insisted that the helicopter fly low, through huge explosions. It flew just a few feet above Vic Morrow and the children.

The result was a tragedy. The violent explosions sent the helicopter spinning out of control. Its blades slicing the air, the helicopter crashed. It landed on Vic Morrow and the children,

Crews clean up the wreckage of the helicopter that crashed on the set of *The Twilight Zone*.

killing all three of them. John Landis was brought to trial for his reckless actions. A jury found him not guilty of causing the three deaths. Landis was not punished, but he admitted that he had broken child labor laws.

Steven Spielberg was not responsible for the tragedy of *Twilight Zone–The Movie.* He was, however, the coproducer of the film. In their book *Outrageous Conduct,* authors Stephen Farber and Marc Green argue that it was Spielberg's job to know what was going on. He should have known that children were hired illegally in the making of the film. If that is true, Spielberg failed in his job. He never admitted that failure. Over the years, he has tried to distance himself from the movie.

The next trouble in Spielberg's career involved *Indiana Jones and the Temple of Doom.* Audiences were shocked by the film's violence. Critics had complained earlier that *Poltergeist,* a film Spielberg wrote and produced in 1982, was too violent for young children. *Temple of Doom* included even more violent scenes, such as a man getting his heart ripped out of his chest. Both *Poltergeist* and *Temple of Doom* were very popular with audiences. But protests led

A scene from *Temple of Doom*

Hollywood studios to create a new rating, "PG-13." This rating was for movies that were considered too violent for children under age thirteen.

TROUBLES IN PRIVATE LIFE

During the 1980s, Spielberg's personal life was as rocky as his career. He had begun dating the actress Amy Irving in the mid-1970s. Irving was the daughter of an actress mother and a theater director father. She was seven years younger than Spielberg. She had made her film debut in 1976 in the horror movie *Carrie*. She was nominated for an Academy Award for Best Supporting Actress for her role in

Barbra Streisand's film *Yentl* (1983). At one point, Spielberg and Irving flew to Japan, planning to be married. Before the marriage could take place, however, the couple broke up. Spielberg would not tell his friends what had gone wrong.

In 1980, Spielberg began dating Kathleen Carey, a junior executive in the music industry. Spielberg hoped that he might be able to start a family with Carey, but she broke off the relationship. "I cried for the first time in ages," Spielberg said.

Spielberg then got back together with Amy Irving. She gave birth to their son, Max, in June of 1985. Spielberg said that making *E.T.* made him realize he wanted to have children.

Amy Irving and Steven Spielberg were

Amy Irving and Spielberg

Irving, Spielberg, and son Max

married in November of 1985. The marriage was happy at first. The couple moved into a fourteen-room mansion in Beverly Hills, California. They spent weekends at Spielberg's beach house in nearby Malibu. They did not attend many big Hollywood parties. Instead, they spent their evenings watching films, playing video games, and eating pizza and junk food.

Before long, however, the marriage began to collapse. Personal problems and pressures from their separate careers drove the couple apart. Biographer Douglas Brode thinks it may have been Spielberg's obsession with movies that drove a wedge between him and his wife. "The only time I feel totally happy is when I'm watching films or making them," Spielberg said. The place where Spielberg was the most happy was not at home. It was at his Spanish-style office on the lot at Universal Studios. For Spielberg, filmmaking was still a golden shield against fear and failure—including the failure of his marriage.

Divorce had been the word Spielberg dreaded most as a child, but he found himself saying it. Spielberg and Irving went through a bitter divorce in 1989. Throughout his personal ups and downs, Spielberg devoted himself to filmmaking. He said that he often did his best work when he felt the worst about his personal life.

THE BOY GENIUS

Spielberg was not always easy to work for. He insisted on perfection, from himself and others. Employees who did not deliver top performances were quickly let go. Spielberg could be cold, and he often kept himself apart from his workers. His mother once joked that when people stopped working for Spielberg, they ceased to exist as far as he was concerned.

Spielberg demands top performances from himself and from everyone who works for him.

At the same time, Spielberg was loyal to his friends and generous in giving credit to his coworkers. He has said that he owes much of the success of his films to two key people, editor Michael Kahn and music composer John Williams. An editor is a person who cuts and rearranges film to make a movie flow better. Kahn has edited most of Spielberg's feature films. Williams wrote the music for most of them.

During the 1980s, Spielberg grew as a man and as an artist. On a list of the best Hollywood movies of all time, many people would include *Jaws, E.T.,* and *Raiders of the Lost Ark.* But none of Spielberg's films dealt with serious "adult" relationships. According to author Douglas Brode, "Critics loudly demanded to know if the boy genius would ever become a mature filmmaker."

IT'S A FACT!

John Williams isn't just one of the most popular and successful film composers. He ranks among the most popular American composers of all time. He has written the score, or background movie music, for most of Spielberg's films, beginning with *The Sugarland Express.* He also wrote the score for George Lucas's *Star Wars* series.

6 GETTING SERIOUS

WOULD SPIELBERG EVER be a serious director? As if to answer his critics, Spielberg directed three serious films: *The Color Purple* (1985), *Empire of the Sun* (1987), and *Always* (1989). All of these films were well made, but none of them was completely successful.

THE COLOR PURPLE

The Color Purple is set in rural Georgia, a part of the South, during the period from 1909 to 1937. In the South at that time, many white people felt anger and superiority toward black people. They treated African Americans badly and often hurt or killed them. This racism made life for African Americans difficult and dangerous.

The Color Purple is the story of Celie, an African American woman. As a girl, Celie is raped by a man she believes to be her father. She has two babies whom her father takes away from her. All her life, she wonders if she will ever see her children again. She is forced to marry a cruel older man, whom she calls "Mister."

IT'S A FACT!

The Color Purple was actually shot in North Carolina, not Georgia. Two planeloads of red clay soil from Georgia were flown to the location to make the movie set look like Georgia.

Mister separates Celie from her beloved sister Nettie. Over the years, he hides the letters that Nettie writes to Celie.

What helps Celie survive and grow strong is her friendship with other women. Sophia, a large, powerful woman, shows Celie how to stand up to her husband. Sophia fights her own husband and slugs another woman. And she hits a white man who slaps her and treats her with disrespect. For that act—which racist whites considered a serious offense—Sophia is harshly punished. She is beaten with a pistol, then thrown in prison for eight years.

The "white folks" almost break Sophia's spirit. But her strength and courage return when she sees Celie finally stand up to Mister and call him "a lowdown dirty dog."

The other woman who helps Celie is Shug Avery, Mister's girlfriend. Shug is a beautiful, fashionable woman who works as a blues singer in nightclubs. She teaches Celie to love life. "More than anything, God loves admiration," Shug tells Celie. "I think it [angers] God if you walk by the color purple in a field and don't notice it."

In the end, Celie finds the strength to leave Mister. Mister tells Celie that she will never survive without him. She is just a poor, black, ugly woman, he says. As she drives away, Celie yells back at Mister, "I'm poor, black, I may even be ugly," she says. "But, dear God, I'm here. I'm here!"

Celie is reunited with her two grown children, who have been living with Nettie in Africa. Her son and daughter have been raised with the strength and pride of their African ancestors. In the last scene of the film, Celie and Nettie sit down together at sunset in a field of purple flowers. They play a hand-clapping game that they played as little girls.

THE RIGHT DIRECTOR?

The film was based on the Pulitzer Prize–winning novel by Alice Walker. Many African Americans were troubled by Walker's novel. They felt that it portrayed African American men as monsters. They were just as upset about the film.

Other people supported the book's message. They felt that women, especially black women, had suffered for too many years. Alice Walker was speaking up for women. But many supportive readers thought that Spielberg was the wrong person to turn the novel into a film. Spielberg usually made "fun" movies. They worried he would soften the powerful impact of the book.

Alice Walker

Even Spielberg wondered if he was the right director for the film. "Don't you want to find a black director or a woman?" he asked Quincy Jones, the film's producer.

Jones wanted Spielberg to direct the film for two reasons. First, he needed Spielberg's power. With Spielberg's name on *The Color Purple,* the movie would definitely get made, and it would be seen. The Spielberg name alone would draw millions of viewers to the theaters. Second, Jones knew that Spielberg believed in the project. Spielberg loved Walker's novel and had many ideas about how to turn it into a movie. When Alice Walker met Spielberg, she agreed that he was the right director for *The Color Purple.*

In the end, though, no one was entirely happy with Spielberg's version of *The Color Purple.* The film was beautifully photographed by Allen Daviau, but it seemed almost too beautiful. Daviau and Spielberg created a gentle, romantic view of rural Georgia. Critics complained that *The Color Purple* did not realistically show the difficult life of African Americans. In Spielberg's movie, no one was poor or hungry or forced to work hard. The world Alice Walker created in her novel was much harsher. *New*

Spielberg directs Whoopi Goldberg in *The Color Purple*.

York Times film critic Janet Maslin complained that the movie lacked "realism and grit."

Spielberg did direct some of the strongest adult performances of his career in *The Color Purple*. Actor Danny Glover made Mister a complex, frightening character. The comedian Whoopi Goldberg became an instant movie star through her role as Celie. Talk-show host Oprah Winfrey played proud, fiery Sophia.

Spielberg faced his biggest challenge in presenting the crucial relationship between Celie and Shug Avery (played by Margaret Avery). In Alice Walker's book, Shug and Celie have a love affair. In the film, Spielberg uses hesitant, tender kisses, to hint at the love between the two women. Some critics accused him of backing away from the more adult themes of Walker's book. Spielberg defended himself by saying he was more interested in the love between the women than the sex.

IT'S A FACT!

Spielberg admitted he didn't have the skill to direct the love scene between Shug and Celie as it was presented in the book. He said, "Any woman director would have done that brilliantly. And I was afraid of it."

The novel *The Color Purple* challenges the reader's beliefs. Spielberg's movie is powerful and even shocking in places, but it does not challenge the beliefs of the audience. The film does what Spielberg movies always do—it praises the human spirit. It shows a mother struggling to hold on to her children.

Goldie Hawn's character Lou Jean does the same thing in *The Sugarland Express*. So does Jilian, the mother whose little boy is snatched away by aliens in *Close Encounters of the Third Kind*. Under

Spielberg's direction, *The Color Purple* became another tribute to ordinary people who have the courage to face danger and the strength to overcome hardship.

EMPIRE OF THE SUN

Spielberg's next film was one of his least popular. *Empire of the Sun* was the first Hollywood film to include scenes shot in the People's Republic of China. Spielberg went on location to Shanghai, China. There, he restaged the Japanese invasion of that city during World War II. Spielberg filmed huge crowd scenes for the invasion, using thousands of Chinese extras.

In the swirling crowds, a British boy becomes separated from his parents. The boy, Jim Graham, is forced to spend the war in a Japanese prison camp. He suffers from hunger and exhaustion, but he learns to survive. Jim turns to Basie, a thieving scoundrel, as a father figure. But Basie betrays Jim and abandons him. In the end, Jim is restored to his parents, but he is not the same happy child he once was.

With *Empire of the Sun*, Spielberg again tried to make a serious film. But audiences found the movie gloomy and confusing. The film was based on a novel by J. G. Ballard. It was turned into a screenplay by British writer Tom Stoppard. Both Stoppard and Ballard saw more troubling effects on Jim than Spielberg did. Spielberg could not help seeing the innocence in the boy. As a result, the film seems to contradict itself. It isn't as sad as the writers wanted it. It isn't as hopeful as Spielberg might have wanted it. Spielberg would not let either Jim or his film grow up.

TWO MORE FLOPS

In 1989, Spielberg decided to make a movie about fliers. He patterned his film after an old Hollywood movie called *A Guy Named Joe* (1944). The earlier film was a story about World War II pilots. Spielberg's film, called *Always,* was about modern-day pilots who use their planes to fight forest fires.

Always has tender love scenes and many special effects, but something is missing. The film is exciting when the pilots are up in the air fighting fires. But on the ground, it moves too slowly. One critic thought the film suffered from Spielberg's decision to set the story in modern times. The men and women in *A Guy Named Joe* were wartime heroes. They were fighting for a cause bigger than them. The heroes in *Always* never seem quite so big or so noble.

Captain Hook harasses Peter Pan in Spielberg's *Hook*.

Spielberg followed *Always* with *Hook,* a retelling of the story of Peter Pan. *Hook* was a large and expensive movie. But it was a bit too complicated for children and too childish for adults. Audiences also felt that Spielberg was hitting them over the head with the message that parents should be responsible and loving to their children. Spielberg forgot one of the oldest rules of Hollywood filmmaking–the story comes first. *Empire of the Sun, Always,* and *Hook* were not well received by critics or audiences. Spielberg needed a hit. He had spent $79 million making *Hook.* He thought *Hook* might be his last big film. He was wrong. His next movie cost $65 million dollars, but it was worth it. *Jurassic Park* became the biggest moneymaking movie of its time.

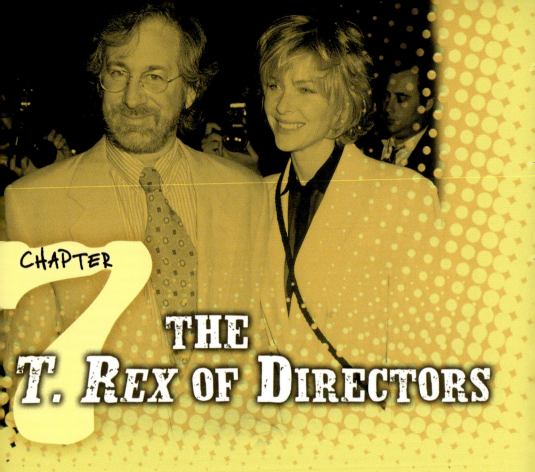

CHAPTER 7

THE T. REX OF DIRECTORS

IN 1991, Spielberg married his second wife, actress Kate Capshaw. Capshaw was one of the stars of *Indiana Jones and the Temple of Doom*. Born in Texas in 1953, she was a schoolteacher before she became an actress. She started her acting career in New York. She acted in television commercials and soap operas before breaking into the movies in 1982. She shares Spielberg's love of movies. She enjoys his constant habit of comparing real-life situations

(Above) Spielberg with his second wife, Kate Capshaw

72

to scenes he remembers from old movies.

> **IT'S A FACT!**
> Kate Capshaw holds a master's degree in special education.

Before her marriage to Spielberg, Capshaw converted to Judaism. It was something she had been thinking about doing for years. Meeting Spielberg and his family convinced her that the time was right. "It was important to me," she said, "to feel as legitimate on the inside as on the outside."

Capshaw says she gets along well with Spielberg's previous wife, Amy Irving. Capshaw and Spielberg are raising a "blended" family. It includes their own children, children they have adopted, and children from their previous marriages. Their seven children are named Max, Theo, Jessica, Sawyer, Sasha, Mikaela, and Destry.

Spielberg says that his wife and family have helped him to understand himself. "Now thanks to Katie and my . . . amazing kids," Spielberg says, "I know who I am without the script."

INFLUENCES

Steven Spielberg has been influenced by many other filmmakers. He watched their movies as a

David Lean *(left)* is one of the directors whom Spielberg *(right)* admired.

child and studied them as an adult. Spielberg has said that the one film that influenced him the most was the ballet film *The Red Shoes* (1948) by British director Michael Powell. Another British director, David Lean *(Lawrence of Arabia* and *Dr. Zhivago),* provided a model for Spielberg's work as a director. Lean's pictures, like Spielberg's, combine close-up stories about people in a larger-than-life event.

Spielberg also has praised the work of the American director John Ford. Ford made 130 films during his long career in Hollywood. (By contrast,

Spielberg had made only 18 feature films by the age of fifty.) Most of all, Spielberg has been influenced by the suspense films directed by Alfred Hitchcock *(Psycho* and *The Birds)* and the children's films produced by Walt Disney Studios.

Walt Disney, who died in 1966, did more than make children's films. He showed that a movie can be the center of a giant sales operation. For Disney, a movie was not simply a story to be told. It was also a rich source of products such as coffee mugs, mouse ears, and Davy Crockett coonskin caps. A movie could become an amusement park ride. It was a chance to "spin off" television shows. (A spin-off is a show that is based on the characters from another show or movie.)

Walt Disney turned his film characters into an amusement park empire that includes Disneyland and Walt Disney World *(right)*.

A movie could be the source for recorded music. For better or for worse, Disney changed the nature of the movie business. He showed filmmakers how to sell hundreds of products based on their movies.

Disney was ahead of his time. Not until the 1970s did other major studios begin to follow his example. George Lucas led the way. He turned his *Star Wars* films into a sales bonanza of toys, T-shirts, and even a ride at Disneyland. By the 1980s, almost every blockbuster film had been designed with the selling of products in mind.

WALT DISNEY

Walt Disney (1901–1966) spent most of his early life on a farm in Missouri. At the age of sixteen, he went to Chicago, Illinois, to study art. By 1920, he was creating cartoons for an advertising agency.

In 1923, Disney moved to Los Angeles to produce and direct films. But he had a hard time making money. His first big success came in 1928, when he released a short film that featured Mickey Mouse. Disney not only directed the cartoon film, he also gave Mickey his voice.

In 1937, Walt Disney Studios released the first full-length cartoon movie. It was *Snow White and the Seven Dwarfs*—the very film that scared Steven Spielberg as a child. Many, many other full-length cartoons and nature films followed. Walt Disney Studios added TV shows to its offerings in the 1950s and opened the first Disney theme park in 1955. Walt Disney World opened in 1971, after his death. Theme parks in Tokyo, Japan, and Paris, France, were added in the 1980s and 1990s.

DINOSAURS

Jurassic Park was in preproduction for two years before actual filming began. Several writers were asked to provide different versions of the screenplay. The story was based on a novel by best-selling author Michael Crichton. Design teams created paintings of the different animals and environments in *Jurassic Park*. Other artists worked with Spielberg to produce storyboards. Three different companies designed full-size, miniature, and computer-generated (CG) dinosaurs for the film. Ideas were continually being tried out and rejected. "It was like survival of the fittest," said production designer Rick Carter.

The years of preproduction paid off when it came time to shoot the film. Spielberg and his crew worked quickly and efficiently. The dinosaurs looked more realistic than anyone had thought possible. Spielberg originally planned to use a combination of full-size and miniature dinosaur models for *Jurassic Park*. A team of workers headed by special-effects wizard Stan Winston created the full-size creatures. They built a twenty-foot-tall *Tyrannosaurus rex* that weighed thirteen thousand pounds. There was even a dinosaur suit that was

Stan Winston created full-size dinosaur models for
Jurassic Park.

worn by an actor. They also created a full-size
mechanical puppet.

Spielberg planned to use miniature models for
about fifty shots in *Jurassic Park*. He turned to the
computer graphics team at Industrial Light and
Magic (ILM), a special-effects company founded by
George Lucas. The ILM team produced believable
dinosaurs, including a CG *Tyrannosaurus rex*. When
the *T. rex* appeared on-screen, ILM's Dennis
Murren said, "Everybody went absolutely crazy. It

was like nothing anyone had ever seen before."
The ILM team had advanced the art of computer
graphics. When Spielberg saw the CG *T. rex,* he
decided to abandon the miniature models that had
been developed for the film. Except for Stan
Winston's full-size creatures, all the dinosaur shots
in *Jurassic Park* were done on the computer.

Much of *Jurassic Park* was shot on soundstages
at Universal Studios in Los Angeles. Several of the
film's major scenes
were created on a
computer. For these
scenes, the
performers had to
act amazed or
terrified even
though they
couldn't actually

The *Velociraptor*
model from the
Jurassic Park exhibit
at Universal Studios

see the dinosaurs. The dinosaurs were added to the film after the humans' performances were shot. Actor Sam Neill plays Dr. Alan Grant. He said that it was sometimes difficult to act awestruck or afraid of dinosaurs that were not really there.

One of the actors, Laura Dern, was asked if Steven Spielberg was a strict or demanding director on *Jurassic Park*. She said, "It's not that he's strict, but that he's so well prepared. He knows exactly what he wants." Dern had expected Spielberg to act like an "important person." She did not expect someone who would spend extra time with the cast and crew.

HURRICANE ON THE SET OF *JURASSIC PARK*

Spielberg chose to shoot the film's location scenes in Hawaii. Filming went smoothly until a day before the end of the shoot. Then Hurricane Iniki struck the Hawaiian island of Kauai. Spielberg and the 140 members of his cast and crew huddled in their hotel's ballroom for seven and a half hours. Winds up to 180 miles an hour raged outside. In fact, a Los Angeles TV station hired Spielberg to report on the hurricane live by phone. He bravely stepped outside when the storm was at full force.

The next morning, Spielberg looked at the damage. The hurricane had uprooted trees and telephone poles. It had blown off roofs and crumbled walls. "Iniki had gone through Kauai like the big bad wolf at the house made of straw," Spielberg said. Fortunately, no one was hurt. By the following Tuesday, shooting had resumed at Universal Studios.

Instead, she said, Spielberg plays and laughs and talks with his cast and crew. "Then he tells us to get back to work," said Dern. "But he never yells."

JURASSIC PARK

As the film begins, the Jurassic Park theme park is not yet open to the public. But already things are going wrong. A caged animal has killed a worker. Lawyers are threatening to close the park before it opens. The park's creator, John Hammond, brings in three scientists to examine Jurassic Park and pronounce it safe. The scientists are stunned to learn that Hammond has filled his park with real, living dinosaurs.

The scientists tour the park, but then the animals break loose. A *Tyrannosaurus rex* stomps on the tour cars. Other dinosaurs kill park workers. With the dinosaurs roaming out of control, the survivors prepare to escape from the park by helicopter.

Throughout the filming of *Jurassic Park,* Spielberg emphasized that the dinosaurs were animals, not monsters. They might be scary, but they should be scary in the way that a hungry lion or tiger is scary. Stan Winston and the other special-effects artists spent months studying the muscles, movements, and sounds of living animals, including elephants, giraffes, and whales.

The director of photography for *Jurassic Park* was Dean Cundey. He said that Spielberg "wanted a very realistic look for Jurassic Park, so that the audience would feel as if they were in the park as much as possible." Cundey and Spielberg succeeded in placing viewers inside a remarkable world. It seemed to bring both the past and the future into the present.

Audiences were thrilled, and *Jurassic Park* took in $900 million at the box office worldwide. More than one thousand products were linked to the film. The film surged ahead of *E.T.* as the biggest moneymaker of all time. Once again, Spielberg proved that he was, in the words of his friend George Lucas, "the *T. rex* of directors."

CHAPTER 8
MAKING SCHINDLER'S LIST

IN 1980, an Australian writer named Thomas Keneally was talking to the owner of a luggage store. The owner, Poldek Pfefferberg, was a Jewish man who had lived through the Holocaust of World War II. Pfefferberg told Keneally that his life had been saved by a German businessman named Oskar Schindler. In fact, Pfefferberg said, Schindler had saved

(Above) **Spielberg and Thomas Keneally, author of *Schindler's List***

the lives of hundreds of Jews. Pfefferberg insisted that Keneally should write a book about this remarkable man.

THE STORY OF OSKAR SCHINDLER

With the help of Pfefferberg and many of the other Schindler Jews, Keneally was able to piece together the story of Oskar Schindler. He published that story in 1982 as the book *Schindler's List.* Steven Spielberg bought the rights to make a movie based on Keneally's book. It took several years before anyone could figure out how to turn the book into a dramatic screenplay. Finally, screenwriter Steven Zaillian wrote a screenplay that Spielberg felt was right. Universal Studios agreed to pay the cost of making the movie, $23 million.

BUYING RIGHTS

When a producer wants to make a movie that is based on a book, he or she must buy the movie rights. Typically, the author has an agent. This person helps the author get the best possible deal—meaning the most money—for the movie rights. Producers also want to get other rights to create tie-in products, such as toys and video games.

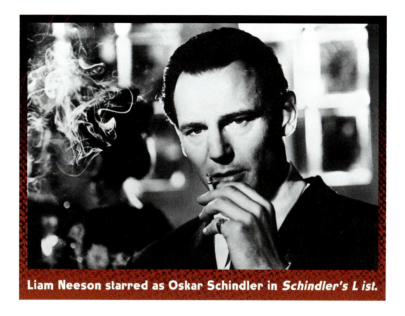

Liam Neeson starred as Oskar Schindler in *Schindler's L ist*.

Spielberg considered using Harrison Ford, the star of the *Indiana Jones* films, to play Schindler. In the end, however, he decided he wanted an actor who was not too familiar with moviegoers. He happened to see the Irish actor Liam Neeson appearing on Broadway in the play *Anna Christie*. After the play, Spielberg took his wife, Kate Capshaw, and her mother backstage to meet Neeson. Neeson noticed that Spielberg's mother-in-law was crying. Apparently, she had been deeply moved by the play. Without even thinking about it, the tall Irishman took this stranger into his arms and hugged her.

Later, Kate said to her husband, "That's exactly what Schindler would have done." Spielberg agreed. Liam Neeson, he decided, should play Schindler.

Spielberg chose Ben Kingsley for the crucial supporting role of Itzhak Stern, Schindler's accountant. Kingsley said that he was deeply affected by the pain and suffering of the Jews in the film. "I

IT'S A FACT!
Ben Kingsley won an Academy Award for his performance in the 1982 film *Gandhi.*

was afraid that the boundaries between actor and role would collapse," he said, "that my colossal grief would make me unable to perform."

A GREAT RESPONSIBILITY

Spielberg himself was torn between powerful emotions and a strong sense of purpose. He wanted to broaden his own knowledge of the Holocaust. So he watched the classic nineteen-hour documentary *Shoah,* by French filmmaker Claude Lanzmann, four times. In the past, Spielberg had forced himself to visit concentration camps. The experience had left him feeling angry and helpless. As he prepared to make *Schindler's List,* he realized he was not

Spielberg and his wife went to the former Nazi death camp at Auschwitz before the filming of *Schindler's List*.

helpless in the face of the Holocaust. There was something he could do to make a difference. He could make a movie.

Spielberg felt a great sense of responsibility. He would make *Schindler's List* for himself. He would make it for the Jews who died in the Holocaust and for those who survived. His gift was the ability to tell stories through film. His duty was to tell this story for Jews everywhere. This time, he would not hide behind the shield of his movie camera. Instead, he would risk his own feelings as a Jew and as a man.

NAZI TARGETS

The Nazis killed about six million Jews, or two-thirds of the Jewish population in Europe in the 1930s. The Nazis also targeted other groups for the death camps, including Gypsies, the mentally and physically handicapped, homosexuals, and people who actively opposed Nazi policies.

To make *Schindler's List,* Spielberg needed all the filmmaking skills he had acquired during his twenty years as a director. *Schindler's List* has large crowd scenes and small, tender moments. The film uses hundreds of actors and tens of thousands of extras. The story spans several years. For important moments in the film, Spielberg backlit his characters. In this way, he used the power of light to draw audiences into a scene. To build drama, Spielberg crosscut, or moved back and forth to show bits of two scenes that were happening at the same time. Most of all, Spielberg used the same dramatic themes he had developed in many of his earlier films. These themes included a hero being rescued from danger; people yearning for the safety of home and family; a man becoming a father figure to people who need him; and a little guy triumphing over wicked, powerful forces.

Schindler's List was filmed quickly. Many scenes were shot with a handheld camera (instead of a steady camera on a stand) so that the film would not look too "polished." Scenes of sudden violence were filmed from a distance, as if the camera just happened to see the action. Cameraman Janus Kaminski said the raw look of the film was intentional. The filmmakers hoped that *Schindler's List* would feel as if it had been made at the time of the Holocaust. To make the film seem older, Spielberg used black-and-white film. Only the beginning, the ending, and one special detail were filmed in color. The special detail was a little girl's red coat.

IT'S A FACT!

The filming of *Schindler's List* began in March of 1993. Much of the film was shot in Poland, where the real story took place.

SCHINDLER'S LIST

Schindler's List opens with a tiny sound: a match is struck to light candles for the Sabbath, a holy day. A Jewish family is gathered around a table, singing a song of worship. As the candles burn down, color fades from the scene. When the last candle goes out, the picture becomes black and white.

The quiet scene is shattered by the noise of a locomotive. It is September of 1939, and Jews from the countryside are arriving at the train station in Kraków, Poland. The new arrivals call out their names. Officials sitting at small tables type their names onto lists. Throughout the film, Nazi clerks make lists of Jews. The Jews are to be rounded up, shipped to concentration camps, and killed.

Oskar Schindler is a German businessman from Czechoslovakia. He has moved to Kraków to make his fortune building kitchen items. He contracts with the Nazi officials to use Polish Jews as slave laborers in his factory. But Schindler, who isn't Jewish, treats his workers as fairly as the Nazis will allow. He feeds his workers well and pays them in valuable pots and pans. Word spreads among the Jews that Schindler's factory is a safe place.

In 1942, a Nazi officer named Amon Goeth comes to Kraków to clear out the area where Jews live. Under Goeth's command, the Jews are rounded up and taken to a labor camp. Those who resist and those who cannot work are shot. Schindler watches the destruction of the ghetto from a hillside above the town. One figure captures Schindler's attention—a little girl wearing a red coat. Later, Schindler sees that red coat after the Nazis have killed the girl and thrown her into a giant pit of dead bodies.

Schindler becomes friends with Goeth, forcing down the disgust he feels for the man. Soon Goeth is ordered to close the labor camp and ship all the remaining Jews to Auschwitz. Schindler offers Goeth a huge bribe. He will pay Goeth to let him take nearly 1,200 Jews to a new factory in Czechoslovakia.

Itzhak Stern types a list of every Jew who works for Schindler. When he is done, he holds up the list. "The list is an absolute good," Stern tells Schindler. "The list is life."

Schindler (Neesom) leans over Stern (Kingsley) as he types what becomes Schindler's list.

Schindler's male workers are brought safely to Czechoslovakia. But the women are mistakenly sent to Auschwitz. As Schindler rushes to their rescue, the women are stripped naked and herded into a shower room. They have heard that the showers at Auschwitz spray poison gas. But this day, the showers spray water. The women are spared. And before they can be gassed by the Nazis, Schindler arrives to take them to his factory. There, the Schindler Jews spend the remainder of the war in safety.

When peace returns, Schindler prepares to leave the factory. His workers gather around him and present him with a gold ring that they have made. The inscription, or saying, on the ring is from the Jewish holy writings called the Talmud. The saying is in Hebrew. Itzhak Stern translates it for Schindler: "Whoever saves one life saves the world entire."

At the end of the film, the image returns to color. We see the real-life Schindler Jews with their children and grandchildren. A subtitle tells us that "there are fewer than four hundred Jews left alive in Poland today. There are six thousand descendants of the Schindler Jews." The Schindler Jews approach the gravesite of Oskar Schindler, who is buried in Israel. As they move past his grave, each of the

Schindler Jews places a stone on the burial marker. Placing stones on a gravesite is a very old Jewish tradition. It is a way of making sure that the winds of time don't sweep away the memories people have of the dead person.

SURVIVORS OF THE SHOAH

Spielberg used his profits from *Schindler's List* to start the Survivors of the Shoah Visual History Foundation. *Shoah* is the Hebrew word for Holocaust. Through the foundation, hundreds of Holocaust survivors have told their stories on videotape. Photographs and other documents are also videotaped. All the tapes become part of a multimedia database. Students can access them through personal computers.

Spielberg calls the Visual History project "a race against time." Most of the Holocaust survivors are sixty, seventy, even eighty years old. Spielberg feels it is important to record their stories before they are gone. Then the stories can be handed down to young people. Through the Shoah Visual History Foundation, memories of the Holocaust will be kept alive. They will serve as a tribute to the survivors and a warning to future generations.

In 1994, Spielberg received the Chaim
Weizmann Philanthropic Leadership Award. At the
award banquet, Spielberg's old mentor, Sidney
Sheinberg, made a speech. He said, "Someday
Steven might be remembered as much for his efforts
on behalf of the welfare of society as for his movies."

Schindler's List was Spielberg's most highly
praised film. Almost everyone thought it was a
gripping movie and a serious work of art. One of
the few who disagreed was J. Hoberman, film critic
for the New York *Village Voice*. Hoberman
complained that Spielberg had made "a feel-good
entertainment about the ultimate feel-bad
experience of the 20th century." The most serious
topic of modern times had been "Spielbergized."

In a way, Hoberman was right. Spielberg could
not help bringing a glimmer of hope to the terrible
story of the Holocaust. Other critics rallied to his
defense, however. So did audiences. Universal had
not expected to make a lot of money with
Schindler's List, but viewers flocked to it. Word soon
spread. This was a film to see.

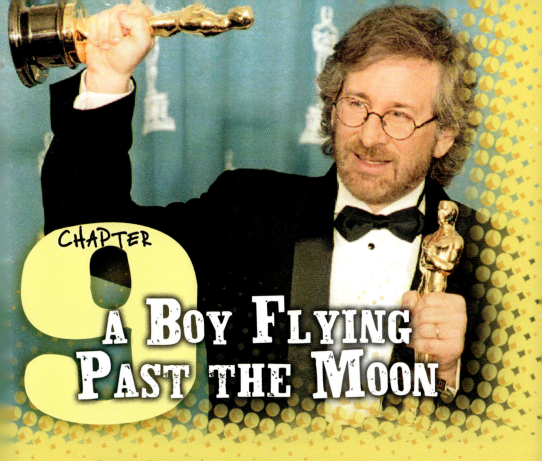

CHAPTER
9
A BOY FLYING PAST THE MOON

EACH SPRING, the Academy of Motion Picture Arts and Sciences presents awards to the top films of the previous year. Everyone in the movie business votes. They pick the year's best movie, director, performers, and other film artists. Steven Spielberg had never won an Academy Award.

Spielberg had always felt that audiences were his "real bosses." They were the people who said whether he had done his job well. But Spielberg still wanted to be recognized by his

(*Above*)
Spielberg with his two Oscars for *Schindler's List*

peers, other filmmakers. He had won awards from the Directors Guild of America (for *The Color Purple).* He had won the 1986 Irving Thalberg Memorial Award for his special contributions to the film industry. But he had not received the biggest Academy Awards– those for Best Picture and Best Director.

Five of Spielberg's films had been nominated for major Academy Awards. *Jaws* and *The Color Purple* were nominated for Best Picture. *Close Encounters of the Third Kind* was nominated for Best Director. *Raiders of the Lost Ark* and *E.T.* were nominated for both Best Picture and Best Director. None of the films had won.

AWARD WINNER AND MOGUL

On the night of the 1994 Academy Awards, Steven Spielberg sat next to his wife and his mother. That night, he finally received recognition from his peers. *Schindler's List* won the Academy Award as the best film of the year. Spielberg was selected Best Director. Holding his award, Spielberg said, "This is the biggest drink of water after the longest drought of my life." He meant he had wanted the award for a long time, and getting it was like getting a drink after being thirsty for years.

Over the years, Spielberg has become a Hollywood "mogul." That means he has wealth and power. As a mogul, Spielberg can make any film he wants. As a producer, Spielberg provides the money and organization to help other filmmakers. He loves stories that appeal to "the kid in all of us." And he likes to help other directors put those stories on film. Richard Donner directed *The Goonies,* a film that Spielberg produced from a story he had written. "Steven is over your shoulder the whole time," Donner said. "He always bows to you because you're the director, but he's got so many good ideas that you want to grab every one of them."

Spielberg has acted as executive producer on several films. These include the animated Fievel films *(An American Tail* and *Fievel Goes West),* the *Back to the Future* series, the two *Gremlins* films, *Men in Black, Men in Black II,* and many others.

In addition to movies, Spielberg has helped to produce several popular television shows. One of those is *ER,* the long-running series about

IT'S A FACT!

ER has won many awards every year, including eight Emmys in its first season alone.

emergency room (ER) doctors. *ER* was developed by Spielberg and *Jurassic Park* author Michael Crichton. It quickly became one of the top-rated shows on television.

STILL A DIRECTOR

Spielberg has much power and responsibility. It would have been easy for him to give up directing and simply run his company. That's what George Lucas decided to do after directing *Star Wars*. He had to deal with huge budgets, thousands of people, complicated equipment, and locations around the world. To maintain control over the many aspects of his films, Lucas became a producer. He left the job of directing to others.

Spielberg was not willing to give up his position as a director. A producer makes the film happen, but a director gives the movie its look and feel. Spielberg has always considered himself an artist. More than anything, he wants to give life to the images and stories he sees in his imagination. Spielberg once said, "Yeah, I'm a mogul now. . . . But when I grow up I still want to be a director."

Spielberg's business partner, Jeffrey Katzenberg, commented on how family life has changed Spielberg. Movies no longer take up every moment of Spielberg's day.

DreamWorks

In October of 1994, Spielberg did something few filmmakers have ever been able to do successfully. He started his own movie studio with part of his $600-million fortune.

Spielberg formed a partnership with two other Hollywood moguls, Jeffrey Katzenberg and David Geffen. Katzenberg was once head of production at Walt Disney Studios. He helped build Disney into the most powerful studio in Hollywood.

The "dream team," from left to right: Jeffrey Katzenberg, Steven Spielberg, and David Geffen

He turned out animated films such as *Beauty and the Beast, Aladdin,* and *The Lion King.* Katzenberg and Spielberg worked together on the production of *Who Framed Roger Rabbit.* And they are partners in a Los Angeles restaurant called DIVE! David Geffen began his career as a music producer. He built his own company, Geffen Records. He also has produced several movies, including *Beetlejuice* and *Interview with the Vampire.*

Jeffrey Katzenberg gave the partners a name that stuck. "This has got to be a 'dream team,'" he said at a news conference. "Certainly it's my dream." Newspaper reporters began calling the partners "the Dream Team." Later, Spielberg suggested they call the studio DreamWorks. Katzenberg and Geffen agreed.

MOVIE STUDIOS

In the whole history of the movie business in Hollywood, only ten major studios were founded. Seven studios—Paramount, Universal, Twentieth Century-Fox, United Artists, Metro-Goldwyn-Mayer, Warner Brothers, and Columbia—are the oldest. Disney started as a very small studio that became major during the last twenty-five years. Only two new studios, TriStar and Orion, were started in the past seventy years. One of those, Orion, is bankrupt.

DreamWorks SKG (*SKG* for *S*pielberg *K*atzenberg *G*effen) produces movies, animated films, television shows, music, and multimedia software. "We're interested in creating a company that will outlive us all," Spielberg said. The new company quickly formed a partnership with Bill Gates. Gates is the president of Microsoft Corporation, the world's most important maker of computer software. With Microsoft, DreamWorks Interactive produces computer games and interactive software.

DreamWorks also signed agreements with ABC television, HBO, and the IBM computer company. George Lucas helped DreamWorks build a state-of-the-art facility for digital editing and special effects.

EARLY DREAMWORKS PROJECTS

In its first few years, the studio's efforts did not meet with great success. Its first film, *Peacemaker* was an action thriller. Audiences were not that interested. They didn't flock to *Amistad,* the first film that Spielberg directed for DreamWorks.

It was only a matter of time before DreamWorks rebounded at the box office. In 1998, the studio had a huge year. It had successes with *Deep Impact, The Prince of Egypt, Antz* and, especially, *Saving Private*

Spielberg gives some pointers to actors in full World War II combat gear during the filming of *Saving Private Ryan.*

Ryan. Spielberg directed this film, a World War II epic starring Tom Hanks. DreamWorks coproduced it with Paramount Pictures Corporation. *Saving Private Ryan* begins with a long, gripping combat scene. The scene was praised as the most realistic battle scene ever filmed. The movie follows a small group of soldiers who must rescue a paratrooper from behind enemy lines. The paratrooper is the last survivor of five brothers sent to fight in Europe.

Saving Private Ryan won five Oscars, including one for Spielberg as best director. Spielberg and Tom Hanks also received the highest honors given to civilians by the U.S. Navy. The Distinguished Public Service Award is given for helping young officers and sailors better understand how to serve their country. With *Saving Private Ryan,* Spielberg had proved once again that he was capable of making serious and powerful movies.

American Beauty was another hit for DreamWorks that won big at the Academy Awards in 1999. The film was awarded five Oscars, including the award for best picture. At the Oscar ceremonies, Spielberg presented the best director award to *American Beauty* director Sam Mendes. Mendes thanked Spielberg for handing him the script. And the film's producers gave thanks to DreamWorks, especially Spielberg. Spielberg had given them the freedom to make a dark comedy about a suburban family.

DreamWorks also found success with 2000's *Almost Famous,* a film about rock bands set in 1973. *Almost Famous* won the Academy Award for Screenplay Written Directly for the Screen. In

IT'S A FACT!

Shrek is filled with famous voices. Mike Myers is the voice of the title role. The voices of Eddie Murphy, Cameron Diaz, and John Lithgow also star.

2001, DreamWorks released *Shrek,* a movie based on a children's book by author/illustrator William Steig. This animated film is about an ogre whose life changes when he meets annoying fairy-tale creatures. It was awarded the first-ever Academy Award for an animated feature film. *(Shrek II* came out in summer of 2004.)

DREAMING FOR A LIVING

Spielberg got back to hands-on work with 2001's *Artificial Intelligence: AI.* He wrote, produced, and directed this film. He also directed 2002's *Minority Report* and *Catch Me If You Can.* DreamWorks released *House of Sand and Fog* in 2003 to glowing reviews from critics and great success at the box office. *House of Sand and Fog* was nominated for three Academy Awards. Spielberg directed *The Terminal,* which came out in 2004. Fans will be happy to know that sequels to some of Spielberg's biggest hit series–particularly *Jurassic Park* and *Indiana Jones*–will be coming out in the mid-2000s.

In the television arena, DreamWorks launched two new series in 2003. *Las Vegas* is a drama about a security force working at one of the biggest

casinos in that city. *Oliver Beene* is a comedy about
a boy growing up in the 1960s.

With these successes, DreamWorks appears to
be living up to its potential to become a major
studio. In addition, Spielberg has linked his Amblin
label to DreamWorks. Over the years, the Amblin
logo has become familiar to audiences around the
world. It tells audiences that a film or television
program was directed by Steven Spielberg or
produced by his company. The logo includes the
famous image from the movie *E.T.*–the outline of a
boy riding a bicycle across the moon. The image
seems to capture the spirit of Steven Spielberg and
his remarkable career. The boy, like Steven
Spielberg, has had the courage to live his dreams. "I
don't dream at night that much," Spielberg once
said, "because I dream all day. I dream for a living."

anti-Semitism: hatred toward Jews as a religious group

backlighting: a technique of lighting a subject from behind it, toward the camera lens, so that the subject stands out clearly against the background

computer generated (CG): a way of creating realistic-looking pictures with computer hardware and software

death camp: a place where prisoners of war are likely to die or be killed. Auschwitz was a Nazi death camp in southwestern Poland during World War II.

"E.T. phone home": a phrase from *E.T. the Extraterrestrial.* E.T. uses the phrase to explain to Elliot why he needs certain things that will enable him to communicate with and ultimately return to his home. In popular culture, the phrase has come to stand for the yearning for home and family.

Holocaust: the almost total destruction by fire of human life. The term mainly describes the Nazi effort to destroy Europe's Jews during World War II. The Hebrew word *Shoah,* which means "extermination," refers to this Nazi program.

Irving Thalberg Memorial Award: given by the Academy of Motion Picture Arts and Sciences to a person whose work is of ongoing high quality. Spielberg received this award in 1986.

meteor shower: an event where Earth passes through the small remains left behind by a comet. The small meteors that can be seen all look like they are coming from the same point in the sky.

Nazi Germany: the name given to Germany from 1933 to

1945, when it was ruled by the Nazi Party. One of the party's stated goals was to eliminate European Jews.

A Night on Bald Mountain: a symphony written by Modest Petrovich Mussorgsky in 1867. Walt Disney used the music in his movie, *Fantasia*. The story behind the symphony is the supernatural activities of witches, demons, and sorcerers during a midsummer's night festival on Bald Mountain.

Survivors of the Shoah Visual History Foundation: a nonprofit organization set up by Steven Spielberg in 1994. Its first mission was to document through videotape the experiences of Holocaust (Shoah) survivors and of those who helped aid or rescue survivors during and after World War II.

World War II: an international conflict that took place in Europe, Asia, and Africa from 1939 through 1945

SOURCE NOTES

7 Douglas Brode, *The Films of Steven Spielberg* (New York: Citadel Press, 1995), 235.

8 Ibid.

11 Philip M. Taylor, *Steven Spielberg: The Man, His Movies and Their Meaning* (New York: Continuum Publishing Co., 1992), 58.

13 Ibid., 51.

13–14 Ibid., 45.

14 Ibid., 22.

14 Ibid., 54.

19 Denise Worrell, "The Eternal Childhood of Steven Spielberg." In *Icons: Intimate Portraits* (New York: Atlantic Monthly Press, 1989), 39–40.

24–25 Brode, 18.

25 Taylor, 62.

28 Ibid., 50.

35 Brode, 53.

39 Dale Pollock, *Skywalking: The Life and Films of George Lucas* (Hollywood, CA: Samuel French, 1990), 68–69.

41 Taylor, 16.

42–43 David Ansen, "Spielberg's Misguided Missile," *Newsweek*, Dec. 17, 1979, 111.

44 Tony Crawley, *The Steven Spielberg Story: The Man behind the Movies* (New York: Quill Press, 1983), 85.

57 Brode, 22.

59 Ibid., 24.

61 Ibid., 162.

66 Ibid., 148.

67 Janet Maslin, "Film: 'The Color Purple,' From Steven Spielberg," *New York Times,* Dec. 18, 1985, C18.

68 Frank Sanello, *Spielberg: The Man, The Movies, The Mythology* (Dallas: Taylor Publishing Company, 1996), 163.

73 James Brady, "In Step With: Kate Capshaw," *Parade Magazine,* Jan. 7, 1996, 16.

73 Elaine Dutka, "On Filmdom's A-List of a Lifetime," *Los Angeles Times,* March 4, 1995, F1.

77 Don Shay and Jody Duncan, *The Making of Jurassic Park* (New York: Ballantine Books, 1993), 56.

78–79 Ibid., 89.

80 Ibid., 43.

80–81 James Brady, "In Step With: Laura Dern," *Parade Magazine,* Oct. 23, 1994, 26.

82 Shay and Duncan, 68.

82 Vernon Scott, "The *T. rex* of directors," *Spielberg Joins Screen Giants.* United Press International, March 3, 1995.

86 Brode, 233.

86 Dutka, F1.

94 "Spielberg Honored at A-List Benefit Event," *Los Angeles Times,* Oct. 3, 1994, E4.

96 Taylor, 12.

97 Donald R. Mott and Cheryl McAllister Saunders, *Steven Spielberg* (Boston: Twayne Publishers, 1986), 146.

98 Taylor, 20.

100 Alan Citron and Claudia Eller, "'Dream Team' Trio Outline Plans for Studio," *Los Angeles Times,* Oct. 13, 1994, A23.

101 Ibid.

105 Worrell, 46.

SELECTED BIBLIOGRAPHY

Basinger, Jeanine. *American Cinema.* New York: Rizzoli, 1994.

Brode, Douglas. *The Films of Steven Spielberg.* New York: Citadel Press, 1995.

Ebert, Roger, and Gene Siskel. *The Future of the Movies,* Kansas City, MO: Andrews and McNeel, 1991.

Hargrove, Jim. *Steven Spielberg: Amazing Filmmaker.* Chicago: Childrens Press, 1988.

Keneally, Thomas. *Schindler's List*. New York: Simon & Schuster, 1982.

Kolker, Robert. *A Cinema of Loneliness*. New York: Oxford University Press, 1988.

Mott, Donald R., and Cheryl McAllister Saunders. *Steven Spielberg*. Boston: Twayne Publishers, 1986.

Sanello, Frank. *Spielberg: The Man, The Movies, The Mythology*. Dallas: Taylor Publishing Company, 1996.

Taylor, Philip M. *Steven Spielberg: The Man, His Movies and Their Meaning*. New York: Continuum Publishing Company, 1992.

Worrell, Denise. "The Eternal Childhood of Steven Spielberg." In *Icons: Intimate Portraits*. New York: Atlantic Monthly Press, 1989.

FURTHER READING AND WEBSITES

Bouzereau, Laurent, and Linda Sunshine, eds. *E.T., the Extra-Terrestrial from Concept to Classic: the Illustrated Story of the Film and the Filmmakers*. New York: Newmarket Press, 2002.

"Cinema." *Annenberg/CPB*.
<http://www.learner.org/exhibits/cinema/>
An overview of the filmmaking process.

Ferber, Elizabeth. *Steven Spielberg*. New York: Chelsea House Publishers, 1997.

Hargrove, Jim. *Steven Spielberg: Amazing Filmmaker*. Chicago: Childrens Press, 1998.

Lawton, Clive A. *Auschwitz: The Story of a Nazi Death Camp*. Cambridge, MA: Candlewick Press, 2002.

Lazo, Caroline. *Alice Walker: Freedom Writer*. Minneapolis: Lerner Publications Company, 2000.

Rubin, Susan Goldman. *Steven Spielberg: Crazy for Movies.* New York: Harry N. Abrams, 2001.

Spielbergfilms.com
<http://www.spielbergfilms.com/>
Information on past and upcoming Spielberg movies.

United States Holocaust Memorial Museum.
<http://www.ushmm.org/>
Learn about the history of the Holocaust as well as current genocide problems.

White, Dana. *George Lucas.* Minneapolis: Lerner Publications Company, 2000.

INDEX

PHOTO ACKNOWLEDGMENTS

Photographs are used with the permission of: Hollywood Book and Poster, pp. 4, 33, 36, 43, 46, 60, 85, 91; © Ralph Dominguez/Globe Photos Inc., p. 10; © Lisa Rose/Globe Photos, Inc., pp. 12, 79; Classmates.com Yearbook Archives, p. 19; Photofest, pp. 20, 27, 56, 67, 102; © Bettmann/CORBIS, pp. 22, 54, 65, 75; © Michael Ferguson/Globe Photos Inc., p. 26; © SUNSET BOULEVARD/ CORBIS SYGMA, p. 32; © Getty Images, pp. 39, 57, 71; © Globe Photos Inc., pp. 41, 78; AP/Wide World Photos, pp. 45, 47; © AFP/Getty Images, pp. 49, 95; Universal/Kobal Collection, p. 51; © David Parker/Globe Photos Inc., pp. 58, 74; © Vincent Zuffante/Star File, Inc., p. 72; © Dave Benett/Globe Photos Inc., p. 83; © Peter Turnley/ CORBIS, p. 87; © Kim Kulish/CORBIS, p. 99.

Cover: © Rufus F. Folkks/CORBIS.